TEST OF FAITH
The Jacob Hochstetler Story

The Heroic, True Story of a
Pioneer Amish Family During the
French and Indian War,
1754 - 1763

Vera Overholt

Illustrated by Annette Durgin

TEST OF FAITH

©Copyright 2007 The Christian Hymnary Publishers
ISBN # 0-9728009-1-3
ALL RIGHTS RESERVED

First Printing 2007
Second Printing 2008

Published by:
The Christian Hymnary Publishers
P.O. Box 7159
Sarasota, Florida 34278
Tel: 941-373-9351
Fax: 941-306-1885

ACKNOWLEDGMENTS

♦ A special thank you to Annette Durgin, for her illustrations and research.

♦ A special thank you also to my daughter, Abigail, for her assistance in the compilation of this book, and to my daughters, Hannah Chupp and Sarah Alimowski, for proofreading the manuscript.

♦ I also wish to acknowledge those who corresponded with me and gave advice or encouragement:

My cousins, Beth Hostetler Mark, author of the book, *Our Flesh and Blood*, and her father, Paul E. Hostetler, both of Mechanicsburg, Pennsylvania;
David Luthy, director of Heritage Historical Library, Aylmer, Ontario;
Daniel E. Hochstetler, Goshen, Indiana, historian and editor of *H/H/H Family Newsletter*.

♦ A thank you also to Sherry Gore, for her counsel and help in typing the manuscript.

FOREWORD

"When the Son of man cometh, shall he find faith on the earth?" (Luke 17:8) It is the author's wish that this story, written for children of all ages, would promote faithfulness and godliness, now, and in the generations to come.

Will we continue to believe and practice all that Jesus teaches in the Sermon on the Mount? (Matthew 5, 6, 7) Or will we drift away with the tide of worldliness in modern "Christianity?"

Will we continue to be a peaceable people who will love our enemies rather than take up arms? "They that take the sword shall perish with the sword" (Matthew 26:52). Will we continue to be a radical, holy people, separate from the world and separated unto God? Will we continue to be authentic Christians and a kingdom of priests unto God? (Revelation 1:7; I Peter 2:5)

Our five children - Nathan, Hannah, Matthias, Abigail, and Sarah - are great, great, great, great, great, great grandchildren of Jacob Hochstetler, the main character of this story. It is my earnest prayer that they and their families, and all of our descendants, would be faithful and continue following Jesus Christ in a distinctive lifestyle.

In writing this story, we have tried to be factual according to historical research. The two main sources are William F. Hochstetler's "Historical Introduction" to *Descendants of Jacob Hochstetler* by Harvey Hostetler, and *Our Flesh and Blood* by Beth Hostetler Mark. Some information comes by way of oral tradition, and some minor details have been added.

I pray that you will discover true faith in God through the pages of this story.

Vera Overholt, Author

INTRODUCTION

Jacob Hochstetler's family were among the pioneer Amish settlers who came to Pennsylvania by invitation of William Penn. Jacob and his wife and children left Rotterdam, Holland, and crossed the Atlantic Ocean on the ship, *Charming Nancy*. Jacob was twenty-six years old when he and his family arrived in Philadelphia, Pennsylvania on November 9, 1738.

Three years later, they moved to the beautiful area of Northkill (now known as Berks County). It was nestled at the eastern edge of the Blue Mountains, which was the western frontier of the British colonies. Jacob and his family worked hard to clear the land and build their large log house and other farm buildings.

Living peaceably around the Amish settlements were Native American tribes (referred to in this story as Indians) and Jacob's home was often visited by them. But that was soon to end. The freedom which drew Jacob and his family to America was threatened by the feuding English and French colonies. Both wanted to claim the land. Caught in the middle, also, were Indian tribes who claimed ownership of the land.

When the war broke out between the British and the French (known as the French and Indian War, 1754-1763), one of their military tactics was to hire Indians to attack, kill, or capture the European settlers in enemy territory. The settlers living on the frontier's edge were especially in danger.

Little did the Hochstetler family realize that their peaceful life was about to be shattered. Would their faith in God sustain them through the greatest trial of their lives?

TEST OF FAITH

"Good night! Be careful!"

"Good night," echoed the young people as they left Jacob Hochstetler's farm to return to their own homes. They walked in groups or rode away on horseback into the dark night. It was September 19, 1757.

The *applesnitzing* was finished. The young people of the little Amish community had been to the Hochstetler's home to peel and cut apples. The apple slices would then be preserved by drying, and stored to eat in the winter months ahead.

The evening had passed swiftly as they worked together "snitzing" apples. Everyone had enjoyed the social event. The Hochstetler family was glad to be a part of a church group that believed in brotherhood and helping each other.

But amidst the enjoyment of the evening was an underlying feeling of uneasiness. Stories had been exchanged of relatives and friends who had been attacked by raiding Indian bands, hired by the French military. Who would be the next target in their war path?

After the young people had all left, the Hochstetlers blew out the lights and went to bed. They soon were sound asleep.

German Prayer

Müde bin ich, geh' zur Ruh',
Schließe meine Augen zu;
Vater, laß die Augen dein
Ueber meinem Bette sein.

Kranken Herzen sende Ruh',
Nasse Augen schließe zu
Laß den Mond am Himmel steh'n
Und die stille Welt beseh'n.

Tired am I and go to rest,
Close my eyes and make request,
Father, may Thine eyes still stay,
O'er my bed till break of day.

Give to broken hearts Thy rest,
Tearful eyes now close and bless;
Let the moon in heaven shine,
O'er this quiet land of Thine.

Translated by John & Vera Overholt

"Arf, arf, arf!" The sound of the dog barking wildly awoke Jacob Jr. Something must be wrong! What was going on?

Jacob Jr. jumped out of bed! He ran to the door and opened it cautiously to see what was the matter. At that moment, someone shot him in the leg! He quickly bolted the door!

Indians! They were being attacked by Indians! Jacob Jr's cry of pain awoke all of the family. They jumped out of their beds and ran to look out the window. They saw Indians and three French Scouts out by the bake oven. The family was terrified!

Jacob's two sons, Joseph, age fifteen, and Christian, age eleven, reached for their guns. They could easily shoot the band of Indians and defend their family!

Though the boys were young, they were skilled marksmen. They had often provided wild game for the family to eat. Wouldn't self-defense be alright in this desperate situation?

"No boys! Don't take your guns!" warned Jacob in an alarmed voice. "Don't shoot! The Bible says we must not kill! We do not want to be responsible for sending anyone into eternity without Christ!"

"But Papa, please. . . We must save our lives!"

"No, we must love our enemies! We *can't* shoot!"

The boys reluctantly laid their guns down and obeyed their father. Now what?

"Jesus answered, My kingdom is not of this world; if my kingdom were of this world, then would my servants fight." Jn. 18:36

"Thou shalt not kill." "Love your enemies, bless them that curse you, do good to them that hate you, and pray for them that despitefully use you..." Mt. 5:21, 44

Suddenly the family realized the house was burning! The Indians had set the house on fire! The family frantically rushed to the cellar. What should they do?

As the fire continued to burn, they thought of the kegs of cider stored in the cellar. "Cider! Here is cider!"

In desperation, they splashed cider on the burning spots of the ceiling to stop the fire from bursting down through the floor above them. What a night of horror!

The day was now beginning to dawn. The Hochstetler family kept on beating back the fire.

The Indians left, thinking the family had all died in the fire. Everything was in ruins!

The Hochstetlers had to get out quickly. They could not stay in the cellar much longer. The smoke was suffocating them!

One by one, they crawled out through a small window. Mrs. Hochstetler had difficulty squeezing through the small cellar window. But they all managed to get free!

But alas! Their freedom and relief soon came to an end! They had not noticed the young Indian, Tom Lions, in the orchard.

The eighteen-year-old warrior had lingered behind and was picking some peaches. Tom saw the family outside and gave a shout to alert the others.

Immediately, his Indian companions were back! Mercilessly they killed the wounded son, Jacob Jr. and his sister and mother.*

Jacob's married son, John, who lived on a farm nearby, had witnessed the tragic scene. He was helpless to come to their rescue. In terror, he hid his wife and child.

Jacob's oldest daughter, Barbara, who also was married, was not at the old home place when the tragedy struck. Imagine her grief when she heard what had happened.

Jacob and his two sons, Joseph and Christian, were taken as prisoners. They walked westward with their Indian captors for seventeen days.

---

* Years before, Mother Hochstetler had harshly refused to give food to some Indians when they had requested it. They drew a rude picture on the outside wall of the Hochstetler's house as they were leaving. This may be why Mrs. Hochstetler was killed in a very cruel way.

It was a long, hard walk across the rugged mountains. Then they rode north by river boat up French Creek to Fort LeBoeuf (present day Erie, Pennsylvania).

When they arrived at the French fort, their Indian captors delivered them into the hands of the French military. What would happen next? Had they suffered so much sorrow and hardship only to be killed by the French?

Soon they learned that the French military had given them to the Indians. When they arrived at the Indian village, the Indians began treating them cruelly.

Jacob and his sons had brought some peaches along, which they presented as a gift to the chief. The chief was so pleased that he ordered that the cruelties be stopped immediately.

Because of the chief's decision, they were spared from running the gauntlet. They had been saved from a lot of torture, which was the customary treatment of captives.

The time soon came when Jacob and his sons were to be separated. Was there no end to their sorrow?

Just before they parted, Jacob turned to his sons and in a pleading voice whispered, "If you are taken so far away and are kept so long that you forget your German language, do not forget the Lord's Prayer."

The Lord's Prayer

9. Unser Vater in dem Himmel. Dein Name werde geheiliget.
10. Dein Reich komme. Dein Wille geschehe auf Erden, wie im Himmel.
11. Unser täglich Brod gib uns heute.
12. Und vergib uns unsere Schulden, wie wir unsern Schuldigern vergeben.
13. Und führe uns nicht in Versuchung, sondern erlöse uns von dem Uebel. Denn dein ist das Reich und die Kraft und die Herrlichkeit in Ewigkeit. Amen.

9. Our Father which art in heaven, Hallowed be thy name.
10. Thy kingdom come, Thy will be done in earth, as it is in heaven.
11. Give us this day our daily bread.
12. And forgive us our debts, as we forgive our debtors.
13. And lead us not into temptation, but deliver us from evil: For thine is the kingdom, and the power, and the glory, for ever. Amen.

Matthew 9

Christian and Joseph were both adopted by Indian families and treated kindly. Jacob, however, was often moved from one Indian village to another. He was not permitted to know where he was.

The Indians painted the white men's faces so that they would look like them. They pulled out Jacob's beard, and cut off most of his hair, leaving only a crown on top. They did the same thing to the heads of Joseph and Christian, too. They made them change their Amish clothes for Indian clothes.

The boys adapted to their new Indian lifestyle, but their father, Jacob, never was satisfied. He longed to go back to his home and to his own Amish people. He thought about trying to escape, but where was he, and where was his home? Which way would he take?

One evening, he saw some older Indians explaining something to the younger ones. They used a stick to make markings in the ashes.

"Oh, a map," Jacob thought. "They're making a map, marking what seems to represent streams and mountains." Jacob tried not to look too interested, but this gave him a slight idea where he was.

During the day, Jacob was sent out to hunt wild game. He returned to the camp every night.

But one day in early May of 1758, he decided to make his escape! The warriors were on a raid, and only the women and children and old men were left at the camp. Now was his chance! They would think he was still out hunting.

That night he did not return to the Indian camp at Buckaloon (near present-day Irvine, Pennsylvania). Instead, he kept on going. It was now seven months since he had been captured.

Jacob was cautious, and ever on the alert so that he would not get caught. He traveled at night and hid during the day. He crossed streams and mountains. Finally, he reached a stream that he thought was one of the head branches of the Susquehanna River.

He continued following that stream. It grew larger! A ray of hope penetrated his weariness and despair.

Now Jacob thought of a plan. He would build a raft and float down the river! He built a raft with logs and tied them together with grapevines. Now he could sit down and rest his weary body as he continued his journey.

Jacob was starving. He ate grass for food. On one occasion, he found a dead opossum with maggots in it. He was so hungry that he ate it.

One night, when Jacob was about to give up, he had a dream. He dreamed that his wife told him he was on the right way and that he should keep going. This gave him renewed courage.

As Jacob floated on down the Susquehanna River, he came near Fort Augusta (what is now known as Shamokin, Pennsylvania). Not far away he saw a man watering his horse! But Jacob was too weak to stand and wave to get anyone's attention. He could barely hold up his right arm.

James Burd, a British colonel who was posted at Fort Augusta, saw in the distance a floating object on the river. He recognized it as a white man on a raft, and rescued him. Jacob was given food and water and a place to rest. How wonderful it felt to him! He was completely exhausted.

He had been on his journey eastward for fifteen days, with little sleep and hardly any food. For four days he had floated on his raft. It was now May 24, 1758. When Jacob felt well enough, Colonel Burd took him by horseback to Carlisle, Pennsylvania. He was examined by Colonel Bouquet about his captivity and escape.

In June, Jacob returned to his home community. He thanked God for a safe return, at last! After he came back, he learned that his former neighbors had sent a petition to Governor Dewey, and had asked him for protection against the Indians. Councils were held between the Whites and Indians to establish peace.

A council was held at Easton, Pennsylvania, from October 8-26, 1758. Governor Dewey and others attended. They agreed to a treaty of peace.

One of the agreements was that the Indians were to bring back all their prisoners and let them return to their families. Governor Johnson would receive them.

About three years later, another council was held, August 3-12, 1761, at Easton, Pennsylvania. The Governor, James Hamilton, attended that one. He said in his speech that very few prisoners were brought back, and the Indians had not kept their promise.

One of the Indians' excuses was that the captives were content and did not wish to leave. The Indians, however, promised again to find and deliver their captives. They agreed to bring them to another council the next summer, which was held at Lancaster, Pennsylvania, in 1762.

Jacob looked forward to the Lancaster meeting, hoping to reunite with Joseph and Christian. But he was deeply disappointed, for his sons were not in the group of delivered captives.

Minutes of Indian Conferences held at Lancaster in August 1762.

> **James Pemberton's Journal (excerpts)**
>
> **The time consumed by negotiating:** *"...about noon the Govr [Hamilton] met with the Indians. Tom King on behalf of the Northern ... Indians spoke & the Conferrence Continued for about 6 Hours, great part seemed to be trifling Ceremony respecting the delivery of the Captives ...."*
>
> **Presentation style of Indians:** *"On Delivering* [a wampum belt] *a noted Warrior of the Seneca Nation (named Cayendah ...) ... quickly laid hold of the Belt and stepped up on a Bench with great Earnestness delivered himself to the foll[owin]g purposes.*
>
>   *Bro[ther]: ... I am a head Warrior & tell the Governor that never shall be another Road, that I have the Care of the Lands & I will keep them for my young Men that are growing up."*
>
> **Translation problems:** *"For want of a Good Interpreter sev[era]l matters were not explained Clearly, it being translated from the Mohawk into Delaware and so into English & so did not afford the desired satisfaction."*
>
> **Interpreters' discretion:** [Following Cayendah's 15-minute speech excerpted above] *"The Interpreter delivd to the Govr but a small part* [of the speech].*"*
>
> **Conversation about return of captives:** *"I heard* [the Seneca Warrior] *mention to One of the fr[ien]dly Germans who was expressing his desire of having the Captives brot in, that he would use his Endeavors, that he had done all the damage & hurt he Could during the Warr, but that as God had now turned his heart he would exert himself as strongly for Peace. But he added he did not take up the Tomahawk until he had 2 of his Own Children ... Killed ..."* (Pemberton, pp. 319-322).

Excerpts from "Journal of James Pemberton at the Lancaster Treaty, 1762," *Indian Treaties* by Benjamin Franklin. This journal was kept by a Quaker merchant, regarding his experiences at the Lancaster Conference.

With the help of a friend, Jacob wrote a petition to Governor James Hamilton to have his sons returned to him. About five years had passed since they were captured and taken away from home.

Not long after the petition to Governor Hamilton, Joseph was returned! Jacob rejoiced to be reunited with Joseph. If only Christian could be home, too!

Several years passed, and Christian was still missing! Who could help Jacob get his son back?

Maybe he could contact Samuel Weiser to help him! Samuel Weiser, at age 16, had been adopted into a Mohawk Indian family. That had been arranged by his father, Conrad, who wanted Samuel to become an Indian agent and interpreter. Surely, he could help Jacob!

Jacob asked Samuel Weiser to write a petition to Sir William Johnson concerning his son. Jacob fervently prayed that Christian would come home.

Sir William Johnson Papers
FROM SAMUEL WEISER
L. S.
[*May 30, 1765*]

[Ma]y it Please Your Exce[llency]
    There is one [Jacob Hochstetler who]
[li]ves in the Province of Pen[nsylvania]
who was up at Fort *Johnson* [   ]
[   ] Joseph home, he being [   ]
[   ] Treaty held about two Years [   ]
[   ] same Jacob Hochstetler would [   ]
[   ] Excellency would be so kind as [   ]
[   ] know if his other Son, *Christian* [   ]
[w]as not brought in by the I[ndians   ]
[   ]t Treaty. He is willing to [   ]
[   ] and Charges and if not [   ]
[   ] would come up to the Mohaw[k   ]
[hi]mself in Order to take him [   ]
[   ] Notice whether his Son [   ]
[   ] come in. I am with [   ]
                Your Excellency's [   ]
                humble Servant
                   [SAMUEL WEISER][1]

ADDRESSED:
To the [   ]
His Excellency
Sir, William Johnson, Baronet
   in the Government of
      New York
Mount Johnson Mohawk Country

---

[1] Indian interpreter, son of Conrad Weiser.

From: Vol. 11, pp. 757-758

PETITION OF JACOB HOCKSTETTER TO GOV. H——, 1762.

To the Hon'ble James Hamilton, Esqr., Lieuten^t Governour of Pennsylvania, &c.

The Humble Petition of Jacob Hockstetler of Berks County.

Humbly Sheweth:

That about ffive Years ago yor Pet^r with 2 Children were taken Prisoners, & his Wife & 2 other Children were kill'd by the Indians, that one of the said Children who is still Prisoner is named Joseph, is about 18 Years old, and Christian is abo^t 16 Years & a half old, That his House & Improvem^{ts} were totally ruined & destroyed.

That your Pet^r understands that neither of his Children are brought down, but the Embassadour of King Kastateeloca, who has one of his Children, is now here.

That your Pet^r most humbly prays your Honour to interpose in this Matter, that his Children may be restored to him, or that he may be put into such a Method as may be effectual for that Purpose.

And yor Pet^r will ever pray, &c.

                          his
               JACOB ⋈ HOCKSTETER.
                        mark.

Aug. 13, 1762.
From: *Pennsylvania Archives* (Series I), vol. 4, p. 99

One day when Jacob was eating dinner, he had an unexpected visitor. The stranger sat outside on a tree stump and waited.

After Jacob finished eating, he went outside to see what his visitor wanted. The tall, young Indian stood and gazed into the White man's eyes. Then he said in broken German, "Ich bin der Christli Hochstetler." (I am Christian Hochstetler.)

Jacob was overjoyed! At last! Christian had come home! God had answered his prayer! Both of his sons were home! Would Christian want to stay with him and Joseph, or would he want to return to his Indian family?

It was harder for Christian to adapt to the White Man's culture and the Amish ways of his family and community, than it had been for Joseph. He could not forsake his Indian friends. Was he Indian or Amish?

Besides this, he had to get used to speaking German again. Even eating at a table seemed strange! The farmhouse was gone, and his mother and sister and brother were gone. Would life ever seem normal again?

It was a difficult struggle for Christian. But after he married his friend, Barbara Rupp, it helped him through the painful adjustments. Yes, he would be a white man again.

Jacob and his sons could never forget the horrors of war. It had completely disrupted their lives. Sorrow and suffering had come upon them because of the selfishness and hatred in men's hearts.

The scars would always be with them. But they could choose to forgive those who had harmed them. Love had overcome evil!

God would do the avenging of the evil doers. He would bless Jacob and his sons for not fighting back.

God had faithfully been with them and shared in their grief. He had carried them in His arms as they walked through the valley of the shadow of death.

Jacob and his family's faith in God had sustained them through the greatest trial of their lives. Their faith had been sorely tested. But if they would remain faithful until death, they would receive a crown of life in Heaven.

The End

"I have kept the faith: henceforth
there is laid up for me
a **CROWN** of righteousness..."
II Timothy 4:7, 8

"When he is tried, he shall receive
the **CROWN** of life, which
the Lord hath promised to them
that love Him." James 1:12

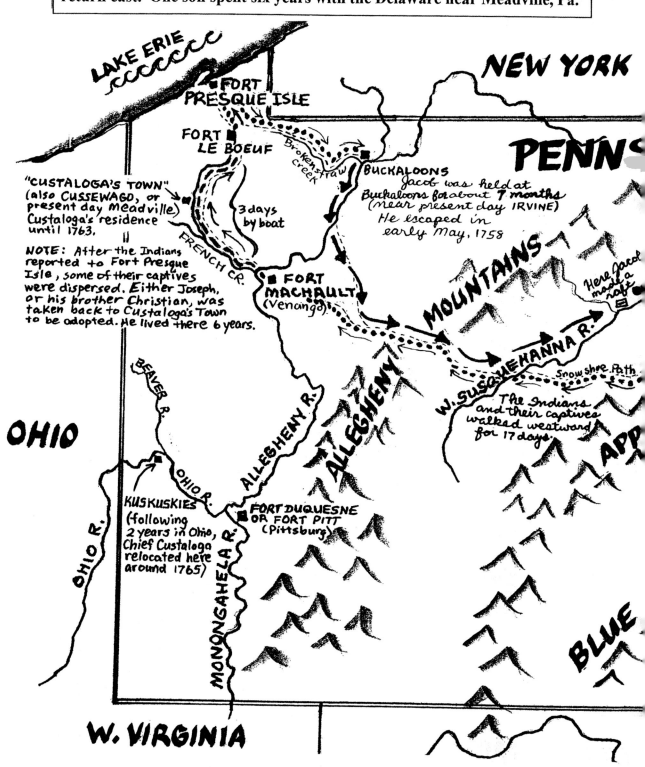

Map drawn by Karen Hostetler Deyhle in *Our Flesh and Blood: A Documentary History of the Jacob Hochstetler Family During the French and Indian War Period, 1757-1765*, Ed. Beth Hostetler Mark. 2d ed. Elkhart, Ind.: Jacob Hochstetler Family Assoc., 2003. Reproduced with permission of editor.

The Statue of Liberty–Ellis Island Foundation, Inc.
proudly presents this

Official Certificate of Registration

in

THE AMERICAN IMMIGRANT WALL OF HONOR

to officially certify that

THE JACOB HOCHSTETLER FAMILY

who came to America from

SWITZERLAND

is among those courageous men and women who came to this country in search of personal freedom, economic opportunity and a future of hope for their families.

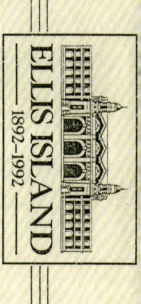

Lee A. Iacocca
The Statue of Liberty-Ellis Island Foundation, Inc.

ADDENDUM I

WHY DID THE AMISH LEAVE EUROPE?

As you reflect on this story, you may wonder why the Amish people came to America. Europe, especially Switzerland, was hostile towards the Amish. Many of them, including Jacob Hochstetler's parents, moved to Alsace, France, where they experienced more tolerance. Jacob's father, also named Jacob, was a fellow-minister with Jacob Amman in Ste. Marie, in Alsace. (Jacob Amman was the founder of the Amish church, which broke away from the Mennonite church).

The Amish were called Anabaptists, which means rebaptizers (Wiedertäufer). They suffered severely because they would not compromise their beliefs and go along with the state church system. Among the beliefs that differed from the state church were the following:

- They believed in voluntary baptism for new believers in Christ (Mark 16:16) rather than compulsory, infant baptism.

- They would not swear with an oath (Matthew 5:34, 37) or take part in the affairs of government. They believed in separation of church and state (Romans 13).

- They strictly believed in the Sermon on the Mount, following Christ in daily life (Matthew 5, 6, 7).

They were a kind, peace-loving, forgiving people, but they were misunderstood and despised by their political leaders and fellow countrymen. They were captured, persecuted, thrown in dungeons, tortured, put to death, or expelled from their towns.

The Anabaptists began immigrating to Pennsylvania, by invitation of William Penn, around the year of 1720. They came to the New World to find refuge in the land of liberty, to serve God in freedom and to live peaceably with all men.

They believed that God created men and women to be choice-makers, and that no authority should force a belief on a person against his conscience. Their desire was to continue following Christ (Nachfolge Christi) without the severe persecution which they endured in Europe.

The New World, however, was not as great as they thought it would be. Here they needed to stand up for truth just as much as in the Old Country. They faced hardships and conflicts due to the Indian raids, the French and Indian War, and the Revolutionary War.

They did not have an easy life, but they had wonderful peace in their hearts. They also had a clear conscience by following Jesus and doing what was right.

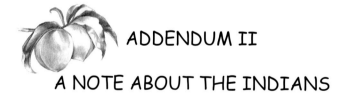

ADDENDUM II

A NOTE ABOUT THE INDIANS

For the most part, the Indians and the Amish got along with each other. As long as William Penn lived, the Indians respected him by not attacking his colony.

But after William Penn died in 1718, misunderstandings arose. It was partly due to the fact that his son, Thomas, had cheated the Indians.

When the French and Indian War broke out in 1754, the Amish settlements also experienced hardships and death. But the Amish did not participate in the war. They believed in Christ's command to love their enemies and not resist evil (Matthew 5:39, 44).

Many of the white settlers were taken captive by the Indians. The children and young people, especially, were treated with kindness and affection, and became a part of their families.

When they were released, some ran back to their Indian homes. According to oral tradition, either Joseph or Christian visited his Indian family after he had been released to go home to his father, Jacob Hochstetler.

During the war, White settlers had killed many innocent Indians out of vengeance for their losses. But the Amish families did not believe in taking the life of another, even to save their own lives. Because of that, many of them fled from Berks County.

Instead of fighting the Indians, they moved to safer locations. Some of the Northkill Amish families moved to Lancaster County, Pennsylvania, around sixty miles south, and started a settlement there. (Today, Lancaster is one of the largest Amish communities in the United States.)

The war ended in 1763 by the Treaty of Paris, seven years after Jacob and his sons were captured. No one would ever be the same.

ADDENDUM III

JOHN J. OVERHOLT'S POEM

The following poem was written by my husband, the late John J. Overholt. He was a sixth generation descendant of Jacob Hochstetler. Can you find your name in this list of descendants? Is Jacob Hochstetler your ancestor, as well?

This poem was first printed in *The Budget* on April 21, 1982. Most of the information was taken from the "Historical Introduction," written by William F. Hochstetler (in Harvey Hochstetler's book, *Descendants of Jacob Hochstetler*). Familiar Amish and Mennonite names are not included since most of them are descendants.

Ode to Ancestor Jacob Hochstetler (1712-1776)

Jacob Hochstetler, probably named after Jacob Amman, the reformer and ancestor of most present-day Amish, has escaped from a three-year captivity with the Indians during the French and Indian War. The year is 1760. On the way home, he builds a raft on the banks of the Susquehanna head waters and, completely fatigued, floats down to Fort Harris (present-day Harrisburg, PA). En route, he reminisces of the murder of his wife, "Miss Lorentz," son, Jacob, and unnamed daughter. He thinks of his three remaining sons, John, Joseph, and Christian, and daughter Barbara. The author, then, has him wonder, too, about unborn generations of descendants living in a place of war and unrest.

1. On the river Susquehanna,
   Near Fort Harris' panorama,
   Now in Harrisburg's urbana,
   Lay a corpse-like figure prone;
   Seventeen-sixty men were writing,
   Indians, Englishmen were fighting;
   His escape he'd made alone.

2. On a log raft tied with grape vines,
   Improvised into ship-shape twines,
   He had charted no escape lines,
   To transport him to his home,
   He could only lie there drifting
   Down the Susquehanna's shifting
   Stream not seeing river's foam.

3. As he drifted he lay pondering,
   Had God heard him he was wondering,
   Now for three years he'd been wandering,
   Captive to the Indian foe;
   From Detroit to Erie walking
   Always moving, seldom talking
   His had been a trail of woe.

4. Dismal was the night of murder
   When the object of his ardor,
   His "Miss Lorentz" left earth's order,
   For her heavenly home above;
   Braving savage rage and cunning,
   He all self-defense was shunning,
   In resignation to Christ's love.

Author's note: Since this poem was written in 1982, more research revealed that Ft. Harris should be Ft. Augusta, and Harrisburg should be Shamokin, Pennsylvania, and Jacob's three-year captivity was less than one year.

5. Now the savages were firing,
   His son, Jacob, fell retiring,
   Christian, Joseph were aspiring,
   To return the Indian fire;
   Yet he would them not be hearing,
   Christians true are suffering bearing,
   Theirs is not to kill in ire.

6. Jacob Hochstetler, our father,
   Counseled all his sons to rather
   Suffer loss than pain the other,
   Following Christ's example here;
   He with family moved to cellar,
   His the lot of Christian dweller,
   To resign to God his fear.

7. Soon the savages were burning,
   Yet they managed to be turning
   Out the fires the house then churning,
   'Till the morning light appeared;
   Finally the familly seeing
   They must leave the house agreeing,
   Faced the foe whom they all feared.

8. Now the savages were killing,
   Jacob fell, a daughter willing,
   Gave her life for Christ, instilling
   Too, in all true lights to be;
   Next "Miss Lorentz," wife and mother,
   Knife and tomahawk would smother
   'Till her spirit was set free.

9. Had Tom Lyons not alerted
   The alarm the foe reverted,
   They the harm might have averted
   And the massacre had flown;
   Yet God's ways are always better
   And we dare not question whether,
   If His will we would have known.

10. Joseph, Christian, and their father
    Now must leave their native heather,
    Burying loved ones they must rather
    Leave to John the oldest son;
    They will follow Indian pathways,
    Indian campfires, Indian tribe-ways,
    Follow till the journey's done.

11. Now our father Jacob drifting,
    Down the Susquehanna drifting,
    On his log-raft slowly drifting,
    Wondering, "Is the journey o'er?"
    Eating 'possum with the maggots,
    Braving all the Indian faggots,*
    Wondering, "Must I suffer more?"

12. As he drifted, Jacob pondered,
    Of the future, then, he wondered,
    Of the three long years he'd wandered,
    What must of his family be?
    Where were Christian, Joseph staying?
    Where was John his home surveying?
    When would he his family see?

13. What should come of his descendants?
    Where would live his close dependants?
    How would fare his independence
    From a war of hate and greed?
    Jacob hardly dreamed of kinfolk,
    Of the unborn stream of infolk,
    Who would share his common need.

14. Families yet unborn and pending
    With a heritage unending,
    In a nation born and blending;
    Much as Abraham of old.
    Jacob hardly saw the future
    Of the families formed by suture,
    In a way we now unfold.

* Author's Note: Faggots referred to here are pieces of wood or iron used for fighting.

15. Did he see descendants unborn:
    Adams, Aishe, Allen, Aliman,
    Andrews, Arehart, Armbrust, Arnell,
    Arnold, Aubley, Averitt, Ash;
    Aug, Baer, Babbage, Bagenstose,
    Bailey, Bain, Bair, Baker, Balmer,
    Baltzley, Bandy, Bardo, Barnes.

16. Barnett, Barnhouse, Barren, Basom,
    Batten, Baumgardner, Beal, Beasley,
    Beam, Beck, Beckler,
    Beekley, Beight;
    Beights, Berg, Benell, Berkey, Berkley,
    Bensinger, Blake, Bickel, Bickley,
    Biddle, Bingell, Bittner, Blough,

17. Bixler, Blackburn, Blocher, Blucker,
    Bluebaugh, Bollman, Boruff,
    Boggs, Boor,
    Bower, Bowers, Bowyer, Boyts;
    Bradshaw, Brady, Brandon, Bratton,
    Brendly, Brenton, Briskey,
    Brant, Briggs,
    Bristow, Brooks, Brown, Bridgewater.

18. Burfield, Burger, Burkey, Burkhart,
    Burk, Burns, Bushong, Caldwell, Calhoun,
    Calvert, Campbell, Canfield, Carr;
    Carris, Carrel, Carrell, Caspter,
    Carpenter, Cassingham, Cauble,
    Chambers, Chastain, Cheatle, Chase.

19. Chickasonz, Chess, Chrissey, Christian,
    Clayton, Clemann, Clark,
    Chiff, Cline, Clipp,
    Close, Cook, Collier, Conner, Coss;
    Conrad, Cooper, Cottrel, Cox, Craft,
    Cramer, Crater, Crimmel,
    Cripe, Croft,
    Cuplin, Curry, Crooke, Daily.

20. Dougherty, Davis, Deifendorf,
    Denison, Deeds, Denny, Dorfer,
    Devens, Dewees, Diller, Dimm;
    Dodwell, Domer, Donges, Dougan,
    Donaldson, Dugan, Duncan, Dunifan.

21. Eaby, Ealry, Edwards, Eggen,
    Egleson, Ellis, Elrod, Emmert,
    Engle, Enyart, Erynestine;
    Ervin, Eshelman, Evans, Everell,
    Fair, Farleman, Farmer,
    Fath, Faunce,
    Feller, Fender, Fetter, Fett.

22. Finzer, Fike, Fish, Ford, Foss, Frazier,
    Foust, Freed, Freel, Freidline,
    Frybarger,
    Gainey, Galvin, Gardinier;
    Gardner, Garlets, Gary, Gearhart,
    Geiger, George, Gates,
    Germain, Gilbert,
    Glassburn, Glover, Glotefelty,

23. Gonter, Goodeve, Goshorn, Grady,
    Graebes, Graves, Glose, Gray,
    Green, Grimm,
    Gross, Gunder, Haffley, Hager;
    Haiston, Hambley, Haney, Harbaugh,
    Harber, Hardman, Hardesty.

24. Harger, Harness, Harper,
    Hang, Harp,
    Harrison, Hartman, Haugher,
    Hart, Hause,
    Hawk, Hawn, Hazen, Hecker, Hay;
    Hedden, Hedglin, Heestand, Hegner,
    Hendricks, Henly, Herbert, Herman,
    Herring, Hess, Hey, Housel, Hays.

25. Howard, Huege, Hume, Hershiser, Hostutler, Huffstetler, Hunsberger, Huffstetter, Huffstutler, Hughes; Huffstutter, Hume, Hummel, Humphrey, Hunsley, Hunter, Hutzell, Immel, Ironsmith, Isely, Jeandrewin.

26. Joder, Johnson, Judy, Kain, Kalp, Kaser, Kane, Kaub, Keiper, Kellar, Kelly, Kendall, Kirch, Kern, Keck; Kessler, Kester, Kieffaber, Klass, Kinslow, Kirby, Klingaman, Klinzman, Knisely, Knopanyder, Kolb.

27. Knowlton, Klingelsmith, Kretchman, Kring, Kuch, Krutsinger, Kuenzli, Kull, LaMont, Land, Lancaster, Larson, Laughman, Leer; Lawson, Lauan, Leib, Lentz, Lewis, Lieghley, Lockhart, Livengood, Lint, Livingstone, Lougee, Loughner, Love.

28. Lower, Luke, Lutz, Lyon, Lyons, Marsh, Marteaney, Marteney, Massey, Master, McCanahay, McClain; McConley, McDowell, McFadden, McIntire,, McIntosh, McKenzie, McKnight, McNeely, McNicol, McRobie.

29. Meese, Mehl, Menser, Messer, Metcalf, Meyer, Mickley, Middaugh, Middlebrook, Millard, Mitchelin, Mogel, Moore; Mohler, Morton, Mowrey, Murphy, Murray, Moose, Neff, Nagey, Neihart, Neis, Nell, Nelson, Newcover.

30. Newkirk, Newlan, Newport, Nickelson, Nittrouer, Nueszly, Noon, Oesch, Ohler, Olinger, Oliver, Orendorf; Opel, Orris, Ostrander, Oswald, Ott, Page, Paden, Parsons, Patterson, Patton, Paulin, Pearman, Payne.

31. Peck, Pence, Penrod, Peterson, Pfleeger, Phillips, Philippi, Phipps, Pfeil, Pickerel, Pike, Pine, Pletcher, Poland, Pirl; Porter, Poyser, Prettyman, Prough, Pool, Ratts, Ream, Rea, Reed, Reid, Reinhart, Rensberger, Reitz, Reynolds, Rhoads.

32. Rheinheimer, Richardson, Rhode, Rhodes, Ridgeway, Riesterer, Riley, Rinehart, Ringer, Rinker, Ripple, Rose; Ritter, Robinson, Roysdown, Runyan, Roes, Rush, Sausman, Sayler, Shaffer, Schemmahorn, Schmid, Schmidt, Schweitzer, Sass.

33. Schultz, Scott, Scoonover, Seaman, Sears, See, Seibert, Seiders, Sellers, Sell, Senn, Sentency, Shafer, Shaffer, Shaw; Shaulis, Shelbourne, Shigley, Shoemaker, Shotsberger, Schreckengast, Shull, Shultz, Shumaker, Sigsbee, Shurtz, Sims, Simpson, Sine.

34. Sipp, Sites, Skiles, Smith
    (George of BUDGET fame),
    Slaughter, Snyder, Solomon, Spencer,
    Speeringer, Spahr, Spilker, Sproal;
    Spoerlein, Stahley, Stamm,
    Stantz, Starner,
    Staub, Staum, Stayrook,
    St. Clair, Steinly,
    Steigleder, Steele, Stevanus.

35. Steinly, Stepler, Stilwell, Stineman,
    Stodghill, Stone, Stout,
    Strahley, Strickler,
    Straight, Strite, Sunthimer,
    Stutesman, Stroup;
    Suttles, Swain, Sturtz,
    Swanger, Swonger,
    Syler, Syron, Suntimer, Sween,
    Sweene,
    Tayland, Taylor, Thompson, Tiney.

36. Thornberg, Tinsley, Toland, Triplett,
    Troutman, Underwood, Urey, Utter,
    Vansant, Vauthrin, Walker, Wahl;
    Waller, Wallick, Walter, Wambaugh,
    Warren, Watson, Weide, Watts,
    Webb, Weimer, Weiser, Welfly, Weiss.

37. Welfly, Wellbaum, Weller, Werner,
    Wetmiller, Wetzler,
    Weybright, Wiegand,
    Wilcoxen, Wilkey, Williams, White;
    Wiltfong, Winegardner,
    Winger, Wogoman,
    Wolfe, Wood, Woods, Work,
    Working, Worral,
    Wortinger, Wotring, Wright,
    Yaist, Yergin,
    Zehnder, Zeiders, Zerfoss, Zink.

38. Jacob drifted down the river,
    Weak, fatigued, he prayed the Giver
    Earnestly that soon be over
    This raft ride through the unkown;
    As he neared Ft. Harris blindly
    God an answer rendered kindly
    Brought deliverance there alone.

39. Near Ft. Harris where the river,
    Susquehanna's forded over,
    There a man his horse did water
    And beheld a strange sight near;
    To the Commandant called over
    With his spyglass this to cover
    And to make a rescue there.

40. Jacob Hochstetler, our father,
    Near death's door could only rather
    Raise his arm up to the ether
    And thus signify his need;
    There they rescued him in gladness
    And him thus removed from sadness;
    May we praise our God, indeed!

    —By John Hochstetler Miller
       Nissley Knepp Wagler Overholt

(Poem by John J. Overholt, printed in
The Budget, April 21, 1982)

ADDENDUM IV

PHOTOS OF JACOB HOCHSTETLER'S PRESENT-DAY HOMESTEAD

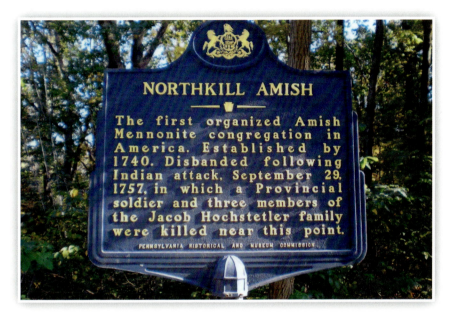

The state of Pennsylvania placed this memorial sign at the end of the lane leading to the present homestead. But the date is wrong; it was September 19.

This may be the original well. It is hand-dug, lined with stones, and near the spring house foundation.

The present house on the Hochstetler homestead is believed to be at the approximate location of the original foundation. Some years later, among the ruins of the fire was found a Franklin stove door, dated 1752.

In front of the house where the bake oven most likely was located.

This monument is on the Hochstetler homestead. It was constructed from the original bake oven stones. This can be seen at Roadside America, (Shartlesville, PA) on Rt. 22 - I 78.

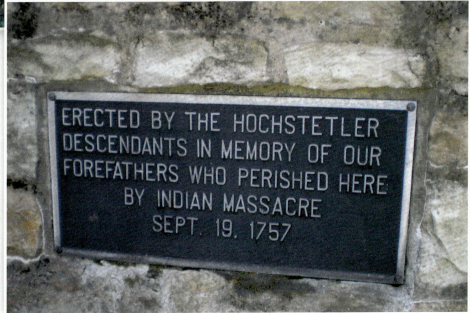

A close-up view of the tribute on the monument.

ADDENDUM V

JACOB HOCHSTETLER'S HYMN BOOK

We do not know all that Jacob Hochstetler brought along to America, but we believe he brought his German Bible and *Ausbund* songbook.

David Luthy of the Heritage Library in Aylmer, Ontario, has seen a European *Ausbund* that appears to have belonged to Jacob Hochstetler. On the back flyleaf of that *Ausbund* is the signature, "jacob hostedler." Another signature on the flyleaf is that of his son, Christian. It says, in German, "This book belongs to me, Christian Hochstetler, 1770."

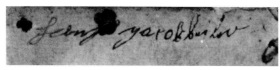

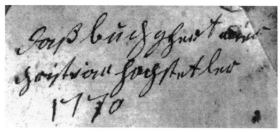

Written on the flyleaf in the back of the Ausbund are twelve lines in fine German script followed by the signature of 'jakob hostedler." Following is a transcription of the writing with an English translation:

gnad fried und ein warhaft-
ige erkanntnuss des gottlichen
worts vermehre sich bei
allen rechten christen und
liebhabern der ewigen
warheit von gott dem
himmlischen Vatter
und jesum christum
unsern herren und selig-
macher durch die kraft
des heiligen geistes amen
filips buch ge?er
    jakob hostedler
	Grace, peace, and a true
	knowledge of the divine
	word be multiplied in
	all true Christians and
	lovers of the eternal
	truth from God the
	Heavenly Father
	and Jesus Christ
	our Lord and Savior
	through the power
	of the Holy Spirit, Amen.
	Philips' book ___?___
	    Jacob Hostedler

(David Luthy, *Family Life*, January, 1988)

We know that everything in Jacob's house was destroyed by fire. But Jacob Beiler, whose signature is on the front flyleaf of that particular *Ausbund*, may have presented it to Jacob.

The *Ausbund* is a collection of hymns written by Anabaptist martyrs while imprisoned for their faith. The original *Ausbund* of fifty-one hymns was first published in 1564. These hymns were written by brethren in the prison at Passau, Germany, in 1535.

Many of the hymns speak of suffering for Jesus' sake. The writers admonish others to be faithful and true. They give accounts of court hearings and heroic deaths.

In addition, the hymns express their Christian beliefs, such as the new birth, holiness of life, separation of church and state, and discipleship (Nachfolge Christi).

The *Ausbund*, which was expanded in 1583 and 1622, is the oldest hymnbook in the world that is still in use today. The German songs are sung by the Amish congregations throughout the United States and Ontario, Canada.

 ADDENDUM VI

TRANSLATIONS OF AUSBUND HYMNS

John J. Overholt, my late husband, translated a number of the *Ausbund* songs into English and set them to rhyme and meter with musical notes. These martyr hymns are compiled in *The Christian Hymnary* (numbers 408-427).

They are written by the following martyrs: Georg Grünwald, Georg Wagner, Georg Blaurock, Leonhart Sommer, Felix Manz, Hans Hut, Johannes Huss, Michael Sattler, Dirk Phillips; also two songs by Menno Simons, prominent Dutch Anabaptist leader; and two songs by Leonard Clock, "Es sind zween Weg in dieser Zeit" (There Are Two Ways in This Our Day), and "O Gott Vater, wir Loben Dich" (O God, Father, Thee We Bless).

The Ohio Amish Library in Millersburg, Ohio, has published a book, *Songs of the Ausbund*. This volume provides literal translations of 69 of the 140 *Ausbund* songs (not set to rhyme and meter). The second volume is forth-coming.

ADDENDUM VII

WHO WAS WILLIAM PENN, AND HOW DID HE HELP THE AMISH IMMIGRANTS?

William Penn was born in London, England, on Oct. 14, 1644. He was the son of Admiral William Penn. When he was sixteen years of age, he attended Oxford University.

While at the university, William Penn rebelled against their rule that everyone must attend the Church of England. He believed that every individual had the right to worship as he pleased.

In 1667, William Penn went to Ireland to manage his father's estates. There he became acquainted with a Quaker preacher, Thomas Loe. It was during the time that the Quakers were being severely persecuted for their faith.

William Penn was greatly impressed with their sincerity and their love for their enemies. He saw they had a faith worth living and dying for, so he joined them also. He was imprisoned three times for writing and preaching about the Quaker faith.

King Charles II, in England, owed William Penn's father a large debt that he could not pay. In 1680, William Penn asked the king to repay the debt with wilderness land in America. His request was granted and the area in the new world was named Pennsylvania, meaning "Penn's Woods."

William Penn made a treaty with the Indians in 1682. It was an unusual treaty. When he purchased the land from them, he did not swear with an oath, because he was a Quaker, and believed in obeying Christ's command not to swear.

He always paid the price they asked for, and then resold the land to the European settlers. His dealings with them were so fair that they did not attack his colony. They got along peaceably together.

Pennsylvania became a place of refuge for his fellow Quakers. He also invited other persecuted, peace-loving groups from Europe to come to Pennsylvania, such as the Amish, Mennonites, and Brethren.*

Thousands responded to the invitation and came to the New World to find refuge. How wonderful it was to own land again and worship God in freedom of conscience!

It was because of these historic, remnant peace-churches that the climate for freedom of choice in religion was created in the United States of America. This influenced the development of The First Amendment.

"The First Amendment was the part of the Constitution of the United States of America adopted in 1788, that guaranteed freedom of religion, freedom of speech, right of assembly; and as such, came to underwrite United States Law as follows:

'Congress shall make no law respecting an establishment of religion, or prohibiting the free exercise thereof; or abridging the freedom of speech, or of the press, or the right of the people peaceably to assemble, and to petition the Government for a redress of grievances.' "

(*That First Amendment and the Remnant* by Leonard Verduin)

*The Hutterites came later, and settled in the western states. They are also a non-resistant, peace-loving group.

ADDENDUM VIII

ANOTHER CAPTIVE RETURNS - REGINA, CAPTIVE GIRL

Regina Hartman, a nine-year-old girl, and her younger sister had also been captured by Indians. The Hartmans were a pioneer, Lutheran family from Germany.

Years later, when the white captives were being returned, Mrs. Hartman went to Carlisle, Pennsylvania, to find her lost daughters. But to her deep sorrow, her daughters were not in the group of released captives.

The second time Mrs. Hartman made the long trip to Carlisle, the same disappointment awaited her. She was heartbroken.

On the third trip she was very discouraged. Would her daughters never be found? She looked carefully at each Indian (white) girl as she walked along the long line of captives. But Mrs. Hartman did not recognize any of them to be her own.

Colonel Bouquet asked Mrs. Hartman if there were any marks on either of the girls that would help her to identify them. No, she did not know of any. He then suggested that she sing a song that Regina might have sung before her captivity.

In a trembling voice, Mrs. Hartman started singing a song they sang as a family long ago, "Allein und doch nicht ganz alleine bin ich." (Alone and yet not all alone am I).*

There was a rustle among the group of captives, and a young lady rushed to Mother Hartman and threw her arms around her neck! It was her daughter, Regina! She had been found at last! What a happy reunion!

It took awhile for Regina to get used to her home again, including the culture and the German language. But as time went on, she unfolded her story and also told of the death of her younger sister.

(*Regina, the German Captive.* Out of print.)

*This song is on page 314 in the *Lieder Sammlung,* which many of the Amish congregations use in their worship services today.

ADDENDUM IX

SOME QUESTIONS PEOPLE ASK US

Q. Who are you?

A. We are members of the Christian church known as Amish Mennonite. The Mennonites originated with Menno Simons of Holland, an Anabaptist reformer (1496-1561). The Amish arose 150 years later, under the reformer, Jacob Amman (1644-1710?). The Anabaptists are the bridge directly to the ancient, apostolic church and have continued the apostolic doctrine of Jesus throughout history.

Q. Why do you dress that way?

A. Because God's word requires modesty, separation, economy, sex-distinction and other Bible principles relative to Christian attire (1 Tim. 2:9, 1 Pet. 3:3-4, Deut. 22:5, Gen. 3:21).

Q. Why do the ladies wear the head veiling?

A. The women's veiling is the ancient Christian teaching taught in 1 Corinthians 11, and it has been worn by Christians since the days of the apostles. It shows women's obedience and subjection to God's Biblical order of headship—God, Christ, man, woman.

Q. What do you believe?

A. We believe all the principles of ancient, historic Christianity, such as the divinity and trinity of God (Mt. 28:19; John 1:1; 15:26), that man is lost in sin, that Jesus is the Saviour from sin, and that the Holy Spirit and the Bible, God's Word, are agents in helping to turn man from sin to a life of holiness and service to God. We believe, further, that the Christian church is made up of born again, holy people (1 Pet. 2:9) that Jesus Christ is the Head of the Church, and that He is personally coming again to take His Church, the people of Jesus, into heaven (Eph. 4; John 14:3).

Jesus will, at the end of time, conduct the judgment of all men, and unrepentant sinners will find their abode separated from God, forever in hell (Mt. 25).

A. We further believe:
- In the inspiration of the Bible (2 Tim. 3:16; Jn. 1:1, 14; Heb. 4:12).
- In a strict separation of church and state as "strangers and pilgrims" (1 Pet. 2:11, 12; Jn. 18:36; 1 Pet. 2:5, 9; Rom. 13).
- In believers' baptism, not infants or children (Mark 16:16; Acts 2:38).
- In love for enemies, non-resistance to evil, non-participation in war (Mt. 5:38-44).
- That the Lord's supper - communion - is to be observed (1 Cor. 11:20-34).
- That washing feet in humility is to be practiced (Jn. 13:1-16).
- That the sick may ask for prayer and anointing with oil (Ja. 5:13-16).
- That God created the world in six literal days and that the theory of evolution is false (Gen. 1:31, 2:1-3, Ex. 20:11, Rom. 1:20).
- That the Lord's Day is to be kept for worship and rest and not for work (1 Cor. 16:1, 2; Rev. 1:10; Is. 58:13).
- That swearing and oaths are wrong (Mt. 5:34-37; Ja. 5:12).
- That a holy, victorious, blameless life is made possible through Christ, and that there is a distinct difference between the people of God and the world (1 Pet. 2:9; 1 Th. 3:13).
- That it is the Christian's responsibility to share the good news of the gospel with everyone (Mt. 28:19; Rom. 1:16; 11 Cor. 4:3).

Q. What does the Bible say about marriage and the family?

A. God is the Author of marriage, and it can only be between a man and a woman who are not already bound (glued together - as written in the original Greek) in a marriage covenant for life (Gen. 2:18-24; Mt. 19:4-6; Mark 10:6-12; Gen. 24:58, 67). This covenant is watched over by God, and cannot be dissolved until either the husband or the wife dies (Mal. 2:14-15; 1 Cor. 7:39). Any additional marriages while the life-long spouse is living are adulterous marriages (Luke 16:18; Rom. 7:2-3) and must be ended and repented of (Ezra 10:3; 1 Cor. 6:9-10; Rev. 2:22) so that reconciliation with the life-long spouse is made possible and the marriage restored (1 Cor. 7:10-11; Hosea 2:5-23, 3:1-3 NIV).

God has created man and woman with equal value (Gal. 3:28) but He has designed headship order with distinct, separate roles (1 Cor. 11:1-15).

The husband is the head of the wife and is to love her at all times (Eph. 5:23, 25, 28; 1 Pet. 3:7, 8). The wife is to submit to her husband's leadership and is to love her husband and children (Tit. 2:4-5; 1 Pet. 3:1; Eph. 5:22-24).

Fathers are to nurture, teach, and discipline their children in love and not provoke them to anger (Col. 3:21, Eph. 6:4; Heb. 12:9) and children are to obey their parents (Eph. 6:1; Col. 3:20).

Q. May others join your church?

A. Yes, our church is open to all persons who:
   —Receive Jesus as Saviour and Lord (Eph. 2:8; 11 Tim. 1:9-10; 1 Cor. 12; Col. 1:17-19).
   —Follow Jesus in a life of obedience and discipleship (Eph. 5; 1-2, 7-8; Rom. 12:4-5).
   —Accept our standards of practical holiness (Acts 2:42; Heb. 13:17).

Joining our church, however, or any other church, does not make one a Christian. Each one must make a personal commitment to Jesus Christ and be born again.

The following Bible verses will help you:

"Except a man be born again, he cannot see the kingdom of God" (John 3:3).

"The blood of Jesus Christ His Son cleanseth us from all sin" (I John 1:7).

"Repent, and be baptized every one of you in the name of Jesus Christ for the remission of sins, and ye shall receive the gift of the Holy Ghost" (Acts 2:38).

"And we are witnesses of these things: and so is also the Holy Ghost, whom God hath given to them that *obey Him*" (Acts 5:32).

"For God so loved the world, that He gave His only begotten son; that whosoever believeth in Him should not perish, but have everlasting life" (John 3:16).

"And this is life eternal, that they might know thee (God) the only true God, and Jesus Christ, whom thou hast sent" (John 17:3).

"If we confess our sins, He is faithful and just to forgive us our sins, and to cleanse us from all unrighteousness" (I John 1:9).

"That if thou shalt confess with thy mouth the Lord Jesus, and shalt believe in thine heart that God hath raised Him from the dead, thou shalt be saved" (Rom. 10:9).

—John J. Overholt
Altered by Vera Overholt

BIBLIOGRAPHY

1. *Our Flesh and Blood — A Documentary History of the Jacob Hochstetler Family During the French and Indian War Period, 1757-1765.* By Beth Hostetler Mark. Published by Jacob Hochstetler Family Association, Inc. P.O. Box 2085, Elkhart, IN 46515.

2. *Contentment — The Life and Times of Jacob Hertzler, Pioneer Amish Bishop, 1703-1706.* By William McGrath. Published by The Christian Hymnary Publishers, P.O. Box 7159, Sarasota, FL 34278.

3. *That First Amendment and The Remnant.* By Leonard Verduin. Published by The Christian Hymnary Publishers, P.O. Box 7159, Sarasota, FL 34278.

4. "Historical Introduction" by William F. Hochstetler in the book, *Descendants of Jacob Hochstetler.* By Harvey Hostetler.

5. *Trials of the Hochstetler Family.* By John M. Byler.

6. *Theological Themes in the Ausbund.* Unpublished thesis by Joseph Overholt.

7. *The Amazing Story of The Ausbund.* By Benuel S. Blank.

8. "Jacob Hostedler's European Ausbund," January, 1988, issue of "Family Life." By David Luthy.

9. *Hochstetler / Hostetler / Hochstedler Family Newsletter,* Daniel E. Hochstetler, Editor. Jacob Hochstetler Family Association.

Additional Books and Music Published By
The Christian Hymnary Publishers

P.O. Box 7159
Sarasota, Florida 34278
Tel: (941) 373-9351
Fax: (941) 306-1885

The Christian Hymnary $12.90

1000 of the best hymns, songs, and chorales for every occasion. This well-loved hymnbook is used nationwide, and is an excellent contribution to the home and to the church. Includes seventeen Ausbund, Anabaptist-martyr selections, translated into English. Also includes rudiments of music section to help you learn to sing shaped notes. Compiler, John J. Overholt (See next page for a cappella CDs and cassettes of selections from *The Christian Hymnary*, sung by the Overholt Family).

The Reformers and Their Stepchildren $10.95

An impartial study of the beginnings, the beliefs, and the continuity of the "stepchildren" Anabaptists - the suffering church down through the centuries who were neither Protestant nor Catholic. This invaluable study will change your life, and help you rise above your identity crisis to discover who you are.
By Leonard Verduin

The Anatomy of a Hybrid $10.95

To be fully human, a person must be a choice-maker, part of a composite society. A composite society is the by-product of the world-view of authentic Christianity, as opposed to totalitarian governments and monolithic societies, in which there is no room for diversity of conviction and thought. The Anabaptists down through the centuries were choice-makers, and suffered persecution and martyrdom rather than compromise this God-given freedom. How did the Anabaptists differ from Constantine and Augustine? Through this well-documented study, you will discover whether you are a part of the Corpus Christianum (persecuting church) or the Corpus Christi (persecuted church). The complete story that Christian historians miss. By Leonard Verduin

That First Amendment and the Remnant $12.95

This amazing study traces the history of the Remnant Anabaptists, whose insistence on choice-making prepared the way for *The First Amendment* to the Constitution of the United States of America. They believed that God has given authority to two autonomous kingdoms which are at work simultaneously, each having its own mission, the one being sacred (kingdom of heaven), and the other being secular (kingdom of earth) and He does not want the two kingdoms to be mixed or confused; the spiritual kingdom, (body of Christ) is directed toward the salvation of mankind, and the earthly kingdom (civil government) is to keep order in a chaotic society. These Remnant groups were earmarked by suffering, because they chose not to go along with realm-mixing. It was because of the historic, Remnant, peace-churches that the climate for freedom of choice in religion was created in the United States of America, influencing the development of *The First Amendment* - the part of the Constitution adopted in 1788, which guaranteed freedom of religion, freedom of speech, right of assembly; and as such, came to underwrite United States Law. By Leonard Verduin.

Set of Three Leonard Verduin Books..$29.95
Do you know someone who has lost his way in the amalgamation of modern-day Christianity? Challenge your friends to return to the narrow way and discover their true identity as Christ-followers, willing to suffer rather than compromise. Give a gift that will make a difference! Set of three life-changing books by Verduin: *The Reformers and Their Stepchildren*, *The Anatomy of a Hybrid*, and *That First Amendment and the Remnant*.

Scrapbook of Ideas for Christian Workers I, II, and III............................$12.00 - $14.00
Three amazing collections of true stories, inspirational clippings, heart-stirring poems, Bible quizzes, beautiful illustrations, and faith-building posters. Especially designed for teachers and Christian workers. A wonderful resource for home-school mothers. Find inspiration for any occasion. By Vera Overholt

Set of Three Scrapbooks of Ideas for Christian Workers...$34.95
A marvelous gift of encouragement for busy mothers, stressed teachers, and aspiring youth. Topical indexes help you to instantly find something to share on short notice.

Christian Songs and Hymns..$14.00
A multilingual songbook of 100 familiar songs in English, with translations in Russian, Ukrainian, German, Polish, and Spanish. Spread the gospel in song! Compiled by John and Vera Overholt

Be Glad and Sing..$8.00
Children and youth songbook for homes and schools and Sunday schools. Over 150 songs, old and new. Thirty-six translations in German. Compiled by Vera Overholt

Be Glad and Sing A Cappella Cassettes..Set of two $8.00
One verse of every song in the book sung by the Overholt Family. Sing along and learn the songs.

Our Guests..$12.95
Keep track of who comes to visit! A unique guest book, without lines, to provide plenty of room to write or add a photo to create memories. A beautiful gift idea. Padded cloth cover. By Vera Overholt

Contentment - The Life and Times of Jacob Hertzler, Pioneer Amish Bishop, 1703-1786........$10.00
What did the pioneer Amish in America experience? History comes alive in this fascinating, true story of the first Amish bishop and his family in the United States. By William McGrath

A Cappella Singing Cassettes...$8.00
A Cappella Singing CDs...$12.00
Are you tired of not being able to understand the words? Try listening to a cappella singing. These songs will touch your heart and draw your attention to the Lord. Most songs are from *The Christian Hymnary*, sung by the Overholt family and friends.

Shipping and Handling per Book - $3.00 (set of three - $6.00)
Prices are subject to change.